Josephine Pollard

God Made the World

A collection of Bible stories in words of easy reading for little children

Josephine Pollard

God Made the World
A collection of Bible stories in words of easy reading for little children

ISBN/EAN: 9783337393670

Printed in Europe, USA, Canada, Australia, Japan

Cover: Foto ©Lupo / pixelio.de

More available books at **www.hansebooks.com**

GOD MADE THE WORLD

A COLLECTION OF BIBLE STORIES IN WORDS
OF EASY READING FOR LITTLE CHILDREN

BY

Josephine Pollard

*Author of BIBLE FOR YOUNG PEOPLE; HISTORY OF THE NEW
TESTAMENT; HISTORY OF THE OLD TESTAMENT; BIBLE
STORIES FOR CHILDREN; RUTH, A BIBLE HEROINE; THE
GOOD SAMARITAN; THE STORY OF JESUS; THE BOYHOOD OF
JESUS; SWEET STORIES OF GOD; etc., etc.*

Illustrated

The Werner Company

NEW YORK   AKRON, OHIO   CHICAGO

1899

GOD MADE THE WORLD

Far back in the past, more years than you could think or count, God made the world. It did not look at first as it does now, for there was no live thing on it, no men, beasts, or birds, not a bush, tree or plant, but all was dark and drear.

Then God said, Let there be light! And the light came. And God saw the light, and it pleased him, and he gave it the name of Day. And when the day was gone, and the dark came back to stay for a while, he gave the dark spell the name of Night. And God did these things on the first day.

The next day God made the clouds, and the sky in which they were to move; and he gave the sky a name; he called it Heav-en.

Then he drove the wa-ters to one place where they were both deep and wide, and he called the wa-ters Seas, and to the dry land he gave the name of

Earth. And God made the grass to grow up out of the earth, and the trees and shrubs that have fruit on them. And the grass and the shrubs and the trees were to bear seeds, so that when these seeds were put in-to the ground more grass and trees and shrubs would grow there. God did these things on the third day.

And God put two great lights in the sky, the Sun to shine by day, and the Moon to shine by night; and he made the stars, and put each one in its place. And these things he did on the fourth day.

And he made the great whales, and all the fish that live in the sea, and the birds that swim on it, as well as those that fly through the air, and make their nests in the deep woods. And these things God did on the fifth day.

God made the beasts: those that are wild and live in the deep, dark woods, far from the homes of men; and those that are tame and of use to men, and live where men live—such as the horse, the cow, the ox and the sheep. And he made the things that creep on the ground, and flies and bugs that course through the air.

And then God made Man, and told him that he should rule the fish of the sea, the birds of the air, and all else that lived on the earth. And he told man that the fruit which grew on the trees and shrubs should be his food, while the beasts were to feed on

AD-AM AND EVE DRIVEN FROM PAR-A-DISE.

the leaves, and on the grass that was spread out on the earth. These things were done on the sixth day.

The next day God did no work at all, but made it a day of rest.

God made man out of the dust of the earth, and breathed in him till the man breathed and moved, and showed signs of life. Then God made a gar-den for man to live in, where all sorts of trees grew that were nice to look at, and that bore fruit good to eat. And this place was called E-den. And through it flowed a large stream that kept the earth moist.

And God took Ad-am, the man he had made, and put him in the gar-den, and told him to take care of it. He told him he might eat of the fruit that grew on all the trees but one. God said he must not eat of that tree, for if he did he would be sure to die. And all the birds and beasts came to Adam, that he might give them their names. And the names he gave them are those by which they are known to this day.

And God saw it was not good for man to be a-lone; he should have some one to be with him and help him. So he had a deep sleep fall on Ad-am, and while he slept God took out of his side a bone, and out of this bone he made a wo-man. Then he brought this wo-man he had made to Ad-am, and she was his wife.

Now there was in this gar-den of E-den a great big snake. And this snake spoke to the wo-man—as Sa-tan speaks to us—to tempt her to sin.

The snake said: Has God told you not to eat of all the trees in the gar-den?

And the wo-man said that they might eat of all but one; if they ate of that or touched it they would be sure to die. The snake told them they should not die, and that God did not wish them to eat of it for fear they would grow wise, and know more than he thought was good for them.

The wo-man heard what the snake said, and when she saw that the tree was nice to look at and the fruit seemed good to eat, she gave no thought to what God had said, but took some of the fruit and ate of it; she gave some to the man, Ad-am, and he did eat.

In a short time they heard a voice, and knew that God spoke to them. Yet they did not come near him when they heard his voice, but ran and tried to hide from him.

But God spoke once more, and said to the man, Where art thou?

And Ad-am said, I heard thy voice, and my fear was so great that I hid from thee.

And God said, Did'st thou eat of the tree I told thee not to eat of?

And the man said, She whom thou dids't give

me to be with me brought me some of the fruit, and I did eat.

And God said to the man's wife, What is this that thou hast done?

And she told God what the snake had said, and how she came to eat of the fruit, and God was wroth with them all. He said the snake should crawl on the ground and eat dust all the days of its life; and he told the wife she should know what it was to be sick and sad, and should have much grief and care.

And God drove the man and his wife out of E-den, and would let them live no more in that fair place. And he sent an-gels to keep watch, and a sword of fire that would turn in all ways, so that the two whom God for their sins drove out of E-den could not get back to the home they had lost.

And God told Ad-am that as he had paid heed to what his wife said, and did eat of the tree which the Lord had told him not to eat of, the ground should bear no more fruit for him by it-self, as it had done up to this time, and Ad-am would have to work hard all his life to raise food to eat, and when he died he would go back to the dust out of which he was made.

But God told Ad-am and his wife that there was a way by which their souls might live on high when their flesh was laid in the ground. He said he would send One from the sky who would give his life for theirs: that is, he would be put to death for

THE EX-PUL-SION FROM THE GAR-DEN OF E-DEN.

THE OFFERINGS OF CAIN AND ABEL.

their sins. Then if they would turn from their sins, and give their hearts to the One who was to save them, God would not turn his face from them, but when they died they would have a home with him, and have no thought of sin.

So Ad-am went forth to till the land, and he gave his wife the name of Eve. And they made coats out of the skins of beasts.

Ad-am and his wife had two sons: Cain and A-bel. When they grew up to be men, Cain, who was the first-born, took care of a farm; A-bel kept a flock of sheep.

CAIN AND A-BEL OF-FER-ING SAC-RI-FI-CES TO GOD.

They both had bad hearts, and at times would be led in-to sin, just as Ad-am and his wife had been. But when A-bel did wrong he was grieved, and sought to make peace with God. One day he brought a lamb from his flock, and killed it, and burnt it on a heap of stones. And the smoke went up on high.

This act of A-bel's pleased God, for it was the sign that a Lamb was to be sent to the world to save men from their sins.

But Cain kept on in his sins, and paid his vows to God not with a lamb, but with fruit or grain out of the field. This did not please God, and the smoke went not up on high. When Cain saw this he was in a rage, and showed by his looks that he was wroth with God. Yet God spoke to him in a kind voice, and said, Why art thou wroth? and why art thou so cast down?

If Cain did right God told him he would be pleased with his gift; but if he did not do right, the fault was his own.

Then Cain was wroth with A-bel, for he saw that God was pleased with A-bel's gift and not with his. And one day when both of them were out in the field he rose up and slew A-bel, and the blood ran out of A-bel's wounds and sank deep in the ground.

As soon as this deed was done, God spoke to Cain, and said: Where is A-bel?

Cain said, I know not. He is not in my care. Then God, who had seen the crime, and knew just how bad his heart was, said to Cain: What hast thou done? The voice of A-bel's blood cries to me from out the ground."

And God told Cain that for his great sin he should move from place to place, as one who was in fear of his life, and had no home to stay in. And if he should plant aught in the field to bear food, it should not grow well.

THE DEATH OF A-BEL.

Weeds would come up and choke it, or it would bear leaves and no fruit, so that Cain would not have much to eat.

And Cain said if God drove him here and there

on the face of the earth, and would not take care of him, all those who met him would want to kill him.

But God said the man who hurt Cain would have a worse fate. God set a mark on Cain; what kind of a mark it was we are not told, but those who saw it would know it was Cain, and it would bring to their minds that God had said no man should kill him.

Ad-am lived to be an old, old man, and had a large flock of chil-dren, who grew up and were wed, and they went off and made homes, and day by day were folks born in-to the world. When Ad-am died he was laid in the ground and went back to dust, as God had said he should when he went out of E-den.

One of the men who lived in those days was named E-noch. It is said of him that he walked with God. That means that he loved God, and thought of him, and kept near him all the time, and did his best to please him.

And E-noch did not die, but God took him up to be with him while he still lived, just as if he were to take up one of us.

And E-noch had a son whose name was Me-thu-se-lah, who died at a great old age. In those times men lived more years than they do now, but in all the years since the world was made no man has been known to live to be as old as Me-thu-se-lah.

THE GREAT FLOOD; AND A GREAT TOWER

In the course of time, when there came to be more folks in the world, they grew fond of sin. They did not love God, or try to please him. And God was wroth with them, and said he would send a flood that would drown the world, and there should not be any dry land left for men, beasts, or birds to live on.

But though most of the folks at that time were as bad as they could be, there was one good man in their midst, and his name was No-ah.

THE ARK.

And God loved No-ah and told him what he meant to do. And God bade No-ah build an ark.

This was a boat. It was to be made large, with rooms in it, and a great door on its side. And it was to be quite high, and to have a roof on top.

And God told No-ah when the ark was done he and his sons and their wives should go in it.

And he told No-ah to take in with him two of each kind of bird and of beast, and of bug, and of things that crept, and to take care of them in the ark so long as the flood should be on the earth; for all that were not in the ark would be sure to be drowned.

So No-ah set out at once to build the ark; and it took him a great while to build it. When not at work on the ark, he would talk of God, and of his plan to send a flood to wash sin out of the world, and would urge the folks to give up their sins, and lead good lives. But they paid no heed to his words, and went from bad to worse all the time that No-ah was at work on the ark.

When it was done God told No-ah to come in-to the ark, for he saw he was a good man who had done his best to serve him, and to bring the birds and beasts with him. For in a few days he would send the rain on the earth, and all that was left on it would be drowned.

So No-ah did as God told him. And when he and his wife, and his three sons and their wives, and the birds and the beasts, both small and great, had

ANNOUNCEMENT OF THE FLOOD AND BUILDING OF THE ARK.

passed through the great door of the ark, God shut them in.

At the end of a week the rain set in, and did not stop for more than a month. The rain seemed to pour out of the sky, and all the springs, the large and small streams, and the great seas, rose up and swept through the length and breadth of the land. They came to where the ark was, and went round and round it, and rose so high that the ark was borne from its place and set a-float on the great wide sea.

Then those who had paid no heed to No-ah, but had kept on in their sins, were in a sad plight. The flood had come, and they knew now that all that he had told them was true. How glad they would have been to go with him in the ark. But it was too late. They ran in wild haste to the tops of the hills in hopes to find there a safe place. But still the floods rose and rose till there was no place for them to go, and all those not in the ark were drowned, and there was not a bit of dry land in the whole wide world.

But God took care of No-ah, and those who were with him, and kept them safe till the floods went down. At the end of five months the sea had gone down so much that the ark stood high and dry on a mount known as Ar-a-rat. It stood there for at least two months, and at the end of that time the sea had gone down so that tops of high hills could be seen here and there.

And No-ah sent forth a ra-ven, and the bird flew this way and that, but came not back to the ark.

Then No-ah sent forth a dove, that he might find out if the ground was yet dry. And the dove flew here and there in search of green things, but found not a tree in sight, and naught but cold hard rock, and so she flew back to the ark and No-ah put out his hand and took her in.

THE RE-TURN OF THE DOVE.

At the end of a week No-ah sent out the dove once more, and at the close of the day she came back with a leaf in her mouth.

As soon as No-ah saw the leaf he knew that the waves had gone down or the dove could not have found it. And he knew that God had sent the dove back to him that he might know the ground would soon be dry.

In a few days he sent the dove out for the third time, but she did not come back; and No-ah was sure then that the ground was dry, and that God meant that for a sign that he should leave the ark in which he had been shut up so long.

And God spoke to No-ah and told him to come out of the ark, and to bring out all that had been in there with him. And No-ah did so, and he built up a heap of stones as A-bel had done, on which he laid beasts and birds, and burnt them, which was the way in which man gave thanks to God in those days.

And No-ah's heart was full of praise to God, who had kept him, and those who were near and dear to him, safe from the flood, while all the rest of the world was drowned.

And God told No-ah and his sons that they should rule on the earth, and might kill the beasts and use the flesh for food. Up to this time those who dwelt on the earth had lived on the fruits of trees and such things as grew out of the ground, and did not know the taste of meat.

And God told No-ah that he would send no more floods to drown the world as this one had done.

The Great Flood; and a Great Tower.

And he gave No-ah a sign that he would keep his word, so that when No-ah saw it he would have no fear of a flood. And this sign was the rain-bow, which God set up in the sky as a bow of hope to No-ah and to all the world.

No-ah lived for years and years af-ter the flood, and died at a ripe old age.

The tribes of No-ah grew so fast that the world was quite well filled once more.

And you would think they would have been glad to serve God, and to do right in his sight. But their hearts were full of sin, and they went on as those had done who were drowned in the flood.

NO-AH'S SAC-RI-FICE.

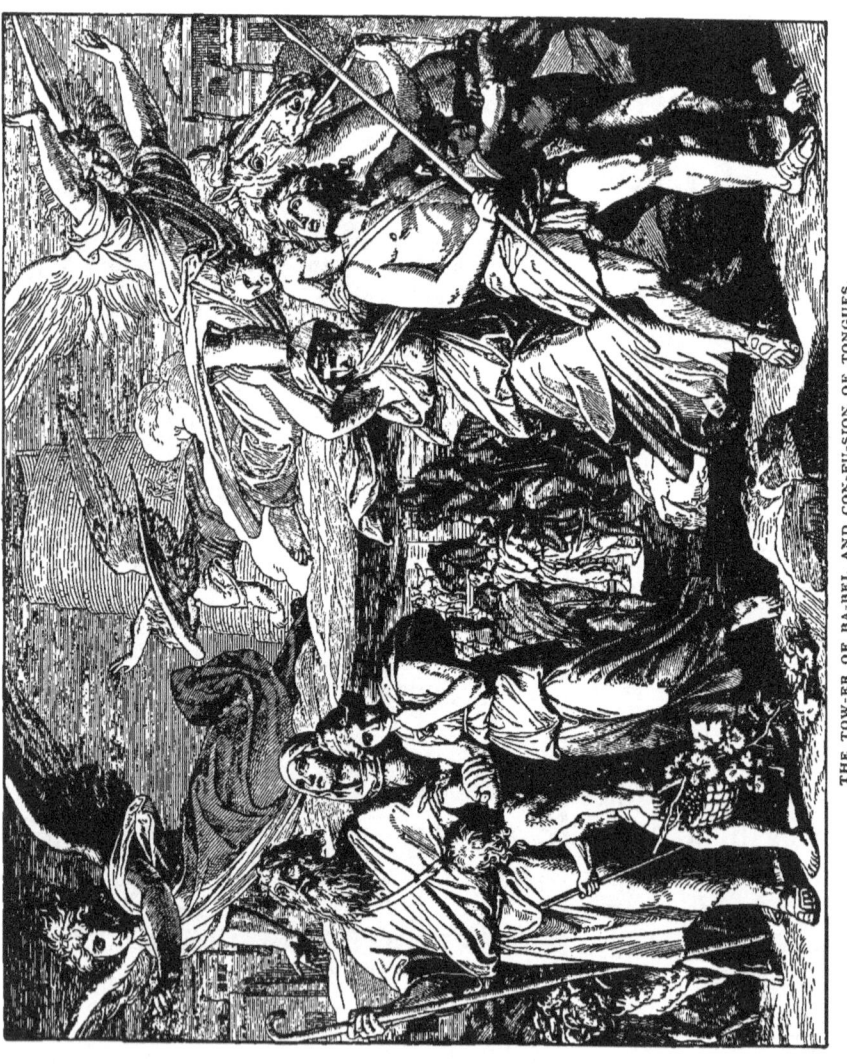

THE TOW-ER OF BA-BEL AND CON-FU-SION OF TONGUES.

The Great Flood; and a Great Tower.

At this time all those who dwelt on the earth spoke but one tongue; that is, they used the same kind of speech.

Now these tribes did not stay in one spot all the time, but would pack up their tents and move from place to place as they chose.

And as they went to the east they came to a plain in the land of Shi-nar. And they said, Let us make brick and build a high tow-er that shall reach up to the sky. And let us make a name, so that when we go from this place it will be known what great men were here, and what great deeds they could do.

And they set to work to build it. God, who read their hearts, knew that sin was at work there, and that the tow-er they meant to build was not to serve him in, or to add to his praise. So he

BUILD-ING THE TOW-ER OF BA-BEL.

was not pleased with their work, and chose a strange way to stop them. He made them all at once speak in strange tongues. This one could not tell what that one said, and they made such a noise that it grew to be just a ba-bel of sound. And that is why it was called the tow-er of Ba-bel.

ABRAHAM: THE MAN OF FAITH

There dwelt in the land of Ur a man whose name was A-bra-ham. And in that land the men did not serve the true God, but had set up false gods to whom they paid their vows.

And God told A-bra-ham to leave his home and go to a land which he would show him. A-bra-ham did not know where the land was, but he had great faith, and knew that God would take care of him and bring him to the land he had told him of.

So A-bra-ham took Sa-rah, his wife, and his bro-ther's son, whose name was Lot, and they set out for the land which God had said he would show him.

A-bra-ham was a rich man, and so was Lot, and they had a great wealth of flocks, and of herds, and of tents. And they each had a large force of herds-men. And these herds-men were at strife.

And A-bra-ham told Lot it was best that they should part; and he said to him, Choose where thou shalt go. If thou wilt take the left hand I will go to the right, and if thou wilt go to the right hand then I will go to the left.

So Lot looked round and saw that the plain of Jor-dan was rich in grass, and would be a fine place for him and his herds to dwell in; so he made his choice at once, and went to live there.

Two large towns were on this plain, Sod-om and Go-mor-rah. The men in Sod-om were full of sin, yet Lot, though a good man, went to live there that he might have a chance to add to his wealth.

As soon as Lot had gone, the Lord told A-bra-ham that he would give to him and his heirs all that land as far as he could see it. And the tribe of A-bra-ham would be so great that no one could count them.

Now Sa-rah A-bra-ham's wife, had a hand-maid—that is, a maid-of-all-work—whose name was Ha-gar; and she came from E-gypt. Ha-gar did Sa-rah a great wrong, and Sa-rah drove her from the house, and she fled to the woods.

An an-gel of the Lord found Ha-gar there by a spring of wa-ter, and said to her, From whence didst thou come? and where wilt thou go? And she said she had fled from Sa-rah, whose maid she was.

And the an-gel said she must go back to Sa-rah and do as she wished her to do. And he told Ha-gar she would have a son whose name would be Ish-ma-el, and that he would live out of doors and be at strife with all men. So Ha-gar went back to Sa-rah, and in due time God gave her a son, who was called Ish-ma-el.

When A-bra-ham was an old man, God told him that he and Sa-rah should have a son, who should be called I-saac.

One day at the hour of noon, when A-bra-ham sat by the door of his tent, he looked up and saw three men quite near him. Then he ran out to meet them, and bowed his face to the ground. And A-bra-ham bade them sit down and rest, and let some wa-ter be brought that they might wash their feet.

No one in those days wore such shoes as are worn now. Some went bare-foot, and some wore just a sole tied to the foot with strings, which did not keep off the dust and dirt as our shoes do.

So when one came in from a long walk the first thing he did was to bathe his feet, as that gave rest and ease, and when guests came the bowl was brought for their use.

Abraham: the Man of Faith.

And A-bra-ham brought them food to eat, and stood by to wait on them; and when they had had their fill, went with them to show them the way.

In those days the Lord came down on the earth and spoke with men, and it is thought that one of these three was the Lord, and the two with him were an-gels.

And the Lord told A-bra-ham that he meant to burn Sod-om and Go-mor-rah for the sins of those who dwelt there.

THE AN-GELS' VIS-IT.

This made A-bra-ham sad, and he said there might be a few good men there, and he begged the Lord to spare the towns for their sakes.

The Lord said he would do so if ten good men could be found there.

And the Lord left A-bra-ham and he went back to his tent. At the close of the day, Lot sat in the gate of Sod-om and two an-gels came there. And as soon as Lot saw them he rose up to meet them and bowed down with his face to the ground.

Then these an-gels told Lot to take out of Sod-om all those who were dear to him, and flee in great haste, as the Lord meant to set the place on fire.

They were told not to look back, but while on their way Lot's wife turned her head, which was a sign that her heart was in Sod-om, and she died where she stood, and turned to salt.

But Lot and his two girls reached Zo-ar at dawn of the next day. Then the Lord rained fire on Sod-om and Go-mor-rah, and they were burnt up in fierce flame, with all that lived there, and all that grew out of the ground.

In due time God gave A-bra-ham the son he had said he should have.

And the child grew, and as soon as it could eat, A-bra-ham made a great feast. And at this feast Sa-rah saw that Ha-gar's son, Ish-ma-el, made fun of her boy, and she begged A-bra-ham to cast him out. A-bra-ham did not wish to do this, but God spoke to him and told him to do as Sa-rah had said,

Abraham : the Man of Faith.

for I-saac was to be the true heir. So the next day A-bra-ham gave food and drink to Ha-gar and sent her and her child out of his house.

And Ha-gar took her boy and went to the waste lands of Beer-she-ba.

And when there was nought for the child to drink, he grew weak, and was like to die. And Ha-gar laid him 'neath a bush and went off and sat down and hid her face, and wept, for she loved her boy very much and did not want to see him die.

DE-STRUC-TION OF THE CIT-IES OF THE PLAIN.

And a voice spoke to Ha-gar out of the sky, and said, What ails thee, Ha-gar? Fear not, for God hath heard the voice of the lad where he is. Rise, lift up the lad and hold him in thine arms.

And the voice told her that her son should be the head of a great tribe. And as she raised her eyes she saw a well of wa-ter, and she ran to it and gave her son a drink and he was soon strong and well once more.

And God was kind to Ish-ma-el, and he grew, and made his home in the woods, and came to have great skill with the bow.

Now it was God's wish to try the faith of A-bra-ham to him.

And he told him to take his son, I-saac, and go to the land of Mo-riah, and lay him on the al-tar he was to build on one of the mounts there. It was not a hard task to kill a lamb, and to burn it so that the smoke of it should rise up to God, like praise from the hearts of men. But how could A-bra-ham take his own dear son, I-saac, and lay him on the wood, and let him be burnt up like a lamb?

Yet God told him to do it, and A-bra-ham knew that it was safe for him to do as God said.

So he rose the next day and took two of his young men with him, and I-saac his son, and cut the wood the right length, and set out for the mount of which God had told him.

And as they drew near the place he took the

HA-GAR AND ISH-MA-EL CAST FORTH.

wood from the ass and laid it on I-saac's back, and took the fire in his hand and a knife, and the two went up the mount.

Now I-saac did not know what the Lord had told A-braham to do, nor why his fa-ther took him up to the mount. And he said, Here is the fire and the wood, but where is the lamb?

And A-bra-ham said, My son, God will give us the lamb we need.

And when they came to the place, A-bra-ham piled up the stones and put the wood on them, and bound I-saac and laid him on the wood.

Then he drew forth the knife to kill his son. And just then a voice from the sky cried out, A-bra-ham! A-bra-ham! And A-bra-ham said, Here am I.

And the Lord told him to do no harm to I-saac, for now he knew that A-bra-ham loved him, since he would not spare his own dear son if it was God's wish that he should give him up.

And as A-bra-ham turned his head he saw a ram that was caught in a bush, and he took the ram and laid it on the wood, and burnt it in-stead of his son.

At the end of a few years A-bra-ham went to live at Heb-ron. And Sa-rah died there.

When I-saac grew up to be a man, A-bra-ham did not wish him to take a wife from the land of Ca-naan where they served strange gods.

Abraham: the Man of Faith.

So he sent one of his men to the land where he used to live to bring back a wife for I-saac.

And as he drew near to a large town in that land he made his cam-els kneel down by a well. And it was the time of day when the wo-men of the place went out to draw wa-ter from the well.

And the man whom A-bra-ham had sent, asked God to help him, and to let him know which one of them was to be I-saac's wife. And he said he would ask one of them for a drink, and if she was kind and gave him a drink, and let his cam-els quench their thirst, then he should know that she was the one God chose to be the wife of A-bra-ham's son.

RE-BEK-AH AT THE WELL.

And he raised his heart to God and said, O

Lord God of A-bra-ham, give me good speed this day.

And while he yet spoke a fair young maid named Re-bek-ah went down to the well and came up with the jar she had filled. And the man ran to meet her, and said to her, Let me drink, I pray thee.

And she said, Drink, my Lord, and held the jar in her hand so that he could drink with ease.

Then she said, I will give thy cam-els a drink; and she went down to the well and drew for all the cam-els. And the man stood still, and was yet in doubt if this was the maid whom God chose to be I-saac's wife.

And as soon as the cam-els had drunk their fill, the man took a gold ear-ring, and two bands of gold for the wrists, and gave them to Re-bek-ah. And he said, Whose child art thou? tell me, I pray thee. And is there room in thy sire's house for us to lodge in?

The maid said that her sire's name was Beth-u-el, and that there was no lack of straw and food, and there was room in the house where he and his men might lodge.

The man was glad when he heard this, for he knew the Lord had led him, and had brought him to the house to which he was sent. And he bowed his head and gave thanks.

RE-BEK-AH JOUR-NEY-ING TO I-SAAC.

The next day Re-bek-ah and her maids went with A-bra-ham's head man. And they came to the land of Ca-naan.

At the close of the day I-saac went to walk in the fields, and as he raised his eyes he saw the cam-els on their way home, and he went out to meet them.

Re-bek-ah said to the man with whom she rode, What man is this that comes through the field to meet us?

And the man told her that it was A-bra-ham's son, I-saac.

Then the maid drew her veil round her so as to hide her face, and came down from the cam-el. And I-saac took her to his house and made her his wife. And A-bra-ham gave all that he had to I-saac; and when he died he was laid by the side of Sa-rah, his wife, in the tomb he had bought at Mach-pe-lah.

And to this day no one has had such faith or trust in God as did A-bra-ham.

JA-COB AND E-SAU

I-saac and Re-bek-ah had two sons. Their names were Ja-cob and E-sau. E-sau was the first-

THE MEET-ING OF I-SAAC AND RE-BEK-AH.

born, and in those days the first-born son had what was called the birth-right. This made him chief of all the rest, and heir to the most of his sire's wealth.

When the boys grew up to be men, E-sau took to the fields and to out-door sports, while Ja-cob was a plain man and dwelt in tents. And I-saac was fond of E-sau, who killed the deer, and brought him the meat to eat. But Re-bek-ah was more fond of Ja-cob.

One day Ja-cob had made some food called pot-tage, and E-sau came in from the field and said, Feed me, I pray thee, with that pot-tage, for I am faint.

And Ja-cob said, Sell me thy birth-right.

And E-sau said, I am at the point of death, so what good will a birth-right do me?

So he sold his birth-right to Ja-cob—which was a wrong thing for him to do—and took the bread and meat, and ate and drank, and then went on his way.

Now there came a time when I-saac was an old man, and his eyes were dim, for he had not long to live. And he called E-sau to his bed-side and told him to go out with his bow and shoot a deer and bring him some of the meat he was so fond of, that he might eat it and bless E-sau ere he died.

And Re-bek-ah heard what I-saac had said to

E-sau, and she told it to Ja-cob. And she said to him, Go now to the flock, and fetch me from thence two good kids, and I will make such a dish as thy fa-ther loves. And thou shalt bring it to him that he may eat, and that he may bless thee ere his death.

So Ja-cob did as he was told, and brought the kids to his mo-ther that she might cook them in a way that would please the good man of the house.

Then Re-bek-ah put some of E-sau's clothes on Ja-cob, and put the skins of goats on his hands, for E-sau's hands had on them a thick coat of hair. And then Ja-cob took the meat and the bread and went in to his fa-ther.

I-SAAC SPEAK-ING TO E-SAU.

And I-saac said, Who art thou, my son?

And Ja-cob said, I am E-sau, thy first-born,

Rise, I pray thee, and eat of the deer's meat I have brought, that thy soul may bless me.

And I-saac said to Ja-cob, How is it that thou hast found it so soon, my son?

And he said, The Lord thy God brought it to me.

And I-saac said to Ja-cob, Come near, I pray thee, that I may feel thee, my son, and know if thou be my son E-sau or not. And Ja-cob went near to his fa-ther and he felt him, and said, The voice is Ja-cob's voice, but the hands are the hands of E-sau.

And he said, Art thou in truth my son E-sau? And Ja-cob said, I am.

And he said, Bring near the food, and I will eat, that my soul may bless thee.

And Ja-cob brought it near to him, and he did eat, and he brought him wine and he drank.

And his fa-ther said to him, Come near now, and kiss me, my son.

And he came near, and gave him the kiss. Then the old man asked God to bless this whom he thought was his first-born, and make him great, and give him all good things.

Ja-cob was scarce yet gone out from his fa-ther when E-sau came in from the hunt. And he brought in a nice dish of meat, and said, Let my fa-ther rise and eat of the flesh of the deer, that thy soul may bless me.

ISAAC BLESSES JACOB FOR ESAU.

JA-COB SEES IN A DREAM THE HEA-VEN-LY LAD-DER.

Jacob and Esau.

And I-saac said, Who art thou?

And he said, I am thy son, thy first-born, E-sau.

And I-saac shook like a leaf, and said, Who? Where is he that took deer's meat and brought it to me so that I did eat ere this, and bless him? Yea, and he shall be blest.

When E-sau heard these words he cried out with great grief, and said to his fa-ther, Bless me too, O my fa-ther!

But I-saac said that he could not take from Ja-cob what was now his—though he had won it through fraud.

And E-sau said in his heart, My fa-ther will soon be dead, and then I will kill Ja-cob.

JA-COB'S DREAM.

And these words were told to Re-bek-ah, and she sent for Ja-cob and said to him that E-sau meant to kill him, and he must leave home at once and go and stay with her bro-ther La-ban till E-sau's wrath had cooled.

And Ja-cob went out from Beer-she-ba.

And as he went on his way he came to a place where he thought he would lie down and rest. The sun was set, the day had been a long one, and he was quite worn out. So he put some stones for his head to rest on, and was soon sound a-sleep.

And while he slept he had a strange dream. He saw a flight of steps that stood on the ground, the top of which was far, far up in the sky. And bright angels went up and down the steps. And the Lord stood at the top, and said, I am with thee, and will take care of thee, and will bring thee back to this land, for I will not leave thee till I have done that which I have told thee of.

And Ja-cob woke out of his sleep, and said, 'Tis true the Lord is in this place, and I knew it not.

And he was in great fear, and said, This is the house of God, and this is the gate of heav-en!

Then he rose up and took the stone on which his head had lain and set it up on end, and he poured oil on top of it. And he gave to that place the name of Beth-el, and made a vow to love and serve God all the rest of his life.

And though he had done wrong, God for-gave him, and he was known as a great and good man.

JACOB AND RACHEL

As Ja-cob went on his way to the East he came to a well that was out in the field, near which lay three great flocks of sheep. And there was a great stone on top of the well. And the men who took care of the flocks would roll the stone from the mouth of the well, and give drink to the sheep. Then they would roll the stone back to the mouth of the well.

Ja-cob said to the men, Whence do ye come?

And they told him.

And he said, Know ye La-ban, the son of Na-hor?

RA-CHEL AND JA-COB AT THE WELL.

And they said, We know him.

And he said, Is he well?

And they said, He is well. And there is one of his girls now, Ra-chel, and she comes this way with her sheep.

While Ja-cob yet spake with the men, Ra-chel came up with the sheep that she took care of. And when Ja-cob saw her, he came near, and drew the stone from the mouth of the well, and gave drink to the whole of her flock.

And as soon as he told her that he was Re-bek-ah's son, she ran home with the news.

And when La-ban heard that his sis-ter's son was near, he ran out to meet him, and threw his arms round his neck and kissed him, and brought him to his house.

And Ja-cob dwelt there for the space of a month.

And La-ban said to Ja-cob, Thou art bone of my bone and flesh of my flesh, but it is not right for thee to serve me for nought. Tell me how much I shall pay thee?

Now La-ban had two girls—Le-ah and Ra-chel. And Ja-cob was in love with Ra-chel; and he said to La-ban, I will serve thee seven years if thou wilt give me Ra-chel for a wife.

And La-ban said it would please him to have Ja-cob for a son-in-law, and Ja-cob served sev-en years for Ra-chel, and they seemed to him but a few days,

Jacob and Rachel.

so great was his love for her. And at the end of that time Ja-cob said to La-ban, Give me my wife, for I have served thee my full time.

And La-ban made a feast, and brought in Le-ah to be Ja-cob's wife. In those days the bride wore a veil, and the man she wed could not look on her face till the next day.

So Ja-cob did not find out this trick till the next morn, and then he came in great wrath to La-ban and said, What is this thou hast done to us? Did I not serve with thee for Ra-chel? and why did'st thou cheat me?

And La-ban said, In our land the first-born must wed the first. Serve me sev-en years more, and thou shalt have Ra-chel for a wife. And Ja-cob did so, and though he dwelt with both—which was thought to be no sin in those days—he was far more fond of Ra-chel than he was of Le-ah.

Le-ah bore Ja-cob a host of sons, but it was years ere Ra-chel had a child. And this made her sad. But at last she had a son, and she called his name Jo-seph. And as soon as Jo-seph was born Ja-cob told La-ban to give him his wives and all the goods that he owned, and let him go back to the land he came from.

But La-ban begged him to stay. He had found, he said, that the Lord had blest him for Ja-cob's sake, and he might have some of the land and the flocks if he would still serve him.

So Ja-cob took care of La-ban's flocks, and had sheep and goats of his own, and things went well for a time.

But one day Ja-cob heard La-ban's sons say some hard things of him, and he saw that La-ban did not give him the kind looks that he used to. And he felt that the time had come for them to part. And the Lord told Ja-cob to go back to the land he came from, and he would deal well with him. And Ja-cob took his wives, and the flocks and the goods he owned, and set out for the land of Ca-naan.

Ja-cob sent one of his men to E-sau to say that he was on his way home, and was in hopes he would find grace in his sight.

And the man brought back word that E-sau was on his way to meet Ja-cob with a large force of men. And Ja-cob thought of the wrongs he had done his broth-er, and was in great fear of him.

He sought the help of God, and God told him what to do. And Ja-cob sent great droves of sheep and goats, and ewes and rams, and camels and colts, and cows, and choice ones from all his live stock, as a gift to E-sau.

And at night, when no one else was near, a man whose face shone with a strange light, came to Ja-

Jacob and Rachel.

cob and wound his arms round him and tried to throw him. And the two strove so hard that Ja-cob's thigh was put out of joint.

And as it grew light the man said, Let me go, for the day breaks.

Ja-cob said, I will not let thee go till thou hast blest me.

And the man said, What is thy name? And he said, Ja-cob.

And he said Thy name shall be no more Ja-cob but Is-ra-el, for as a prince thou hast pow-er with God and with men.

And when he had blest Ja-cob he went his way. And Ja-cob gave the place the name of Pe-ni-el, for, said he,

THE MEET-ING OF JA-COB AND E-SAU.

I have seen God face to face and my life has been spared. For Ja-cob knew by this that E-sau would not kill him.

When Ja-cob was an old, old man Ra-chel bore him a son; and they called his name Ben-ja-min. And Ra-chel died. And it was hard for Ja-cob to have her die and leave him, for his love for her was great, and she was a good wife to him.

JOSEPH AND HIS BRETHREN

Ja-cob had twelve sons, and he was more fond of Jo-seph than of all the rest; for he was the child of his old age. And he gave him a fine coat, and made a great pet of him. This did not please the rest of the sons, and they showed their hate of Jo-seph in all sorts of ways.

One night Jo-seph had a strange dream, and he told it to Le-vi, Sim-e-on, and the rest, and it made them hate him all the more.

He said, As we bound sheaves in the field, lo, my sheaf rose and stood up straight. And your sheaves stood round, and bowed to my sheaf.

And those who heard him said, Shalt thou indeed reign o'er us? And his words and his deeds filled them with a fierce hate.

And it was not long ere he told them of a fresh

dream he had had, in which he saw the sun and moon and e-lev-en stars bow down to him. And he told it to Ja-cob, and his e-lev-en sons.

And Ja-cob took him to task, and said to him, What does this dream mean? Are all of us to bow down to the earth to thee? And he made up his mind to watch these signs, which might be sent of God.

Now Ja-cob had large flocks of sheep and goats at Shech-em, and all of his sons but Jo-seph had gone there to feed them.

JO-SEPH'S DREAM.

And Ja-cob said to Jo-seph, Go and see if it be well with thy brethren, and with the flocks, and bring me back word.

History of the Old Testament.

And Jo-seph went out from the vale of Heb-ron to the land of Shech-em.

When he came there he found that his broth-ers had gone on to Do-than. And Ja-cob went to Do-than and found them. And as soon as he came in

SHECH-EM, THE FIRST CAP-I-TAL OF THE KING-DOM OF IS-RA&L.

sight they thought of a way in which they might get rid of him.

Come, let us kill him, they said; and throw him in-to a pit, and say that a wild beast ate him up. Then we shall see what will be-come of his dreams.

But Reu-ben heard it, and saved him out of their hands. And he said, Let us not kill the lad. Shed no blood; but cast him in-to this pit, and lay no hand on him. For he meant to take him out of the pit, and bear him home to his fath-er.

But when Jo-seph came near these men who should have been kind to him, they took off his coat and threw him in-to the pit, which was dry, or he would have drowned. These old dry wells were left as traps in which to catch the wild beasts that prowled round in the dead of light, and well these bad men knew what would be Jo-seph's fate.

As they sat down to eat, they looked up and saw a lot of men and cam-els on their way to E-gypt, with spices, and balm and myrrh.

JO-SEPH SOLD BY HIS BROTH-ERS.

And Ju-dah—one of Ja-cob s sons—said, Let us not kill the lad, for he is of our own flesh, but let us sell him to these men. And the rest thought it was a good scheme. So they drew Jo-seph up out of the pit and sold him for a small sum, and those who bought the lad took him down with them to E-gypt.

And the bad men took Jo-seph's coat and dipped it in the blood of a kid they had slain. And they brought it to Ja-cob, and said, This have we found. Is it thy son's coat?

And Ja-cob knew it at once, and said, It is my son's coat. Jo-seph has no doubt been the prey of some wild beast. And his grief was great.

The men who bought Jo-seph brought him down to E-gypt and sold him to Pot-i-phar for a slave.

And the Lord was with Jo-seph, who served Pot-i-phar so well, that the rich man put him in charge of his home and lands. But Pot-i-phar's wife told false tales, and Jo-seph, who had done no wrong, was thrust in-to jail. Pha-ra-oh was then king of E-gypt. And it came to pass that he fell out with his but-ler and chief cook, and had them shut up in the same place where Jo-seph was bound.

And the man on guard put them in charge of Jo-seph, who went in and out of the ward as he chose. And one morn when he came in to them he saw they were sad, and asked them why it was.

And they said, We have dreamed dreams, and there is no one to tell us what they mean.

And Jo-seph said, Tell me them, I pray you.

And the chief but-ler told his dream to Jo-seph

Joseph and his Brethren.

first. And he said, In my dream I saw a vine, that put forth three branch-es and brought forth ripe grapes.

And Jo-seph said to him, In three days shall Pha-ra-oh lift up thine head, and put thee back in thy place, and thou shalt serve him as of old. But think of me when it shall be well with thee; speak of me to the king, and bring me out of this house.

And the but-ler said that he would.

Then the chief cook told his dream; and he said, In my dream I had three white bas-kets on my head. And in the top one were all sorts of bake meats for the king. And the birds did eat out of the bas-ket that I bore on my head.

JO-SEPH'S COAT.

And Jo-seph said to him, In three days shall Pha-ra-oh lift up thy head and hang thee on a tree; and the birds shall eat the flesh from thy bones.

The third day was the king's birth-day, and he made a great feast. And he put the chief but-ler back in his place, and hung the chief cook; just as Jo-seph had said he would do. But the chief but-ler gave not a thought to Jo-seph, nor spoke one good word for him to the king, as he had said he would.

Two years from this time the king had a dream, from which he woke, and then fell asleep and dreamt the self-same dream. This was such a strange thing that it made the king feel ill at ease. And he sent for all the wise men in the land to tell him what these dreams meant.

Then the chief but-ler spoke to the king, and said that when he and the cook were in jail, there was a young man there, a Jew, whom the chief of the guard made much use of. And we told him our dreams, and he told us what they meant. And it came out just as he said.

Then the king sent at once for Jo-seph, and said to him: In my dream I stood on the bank of the Nile. And there came up out of the riv-er seven fat cows, and they fed in a field near by. Then sev-en lean cows came up that were naught but skin and bone. And the lean cows ate up the fat cows. And yet no one would have known it, for they were just as lean as when I first saw them. Then I woke, but soon fell a-sleep once more.

Then I dreamt, and in my dream I saw sev-en ears of corn come up on one stalk, full and good. And lo, sev-en ears that were thin and dried up with the east wind sprang up af-ter them. And the poor ears ate up the good ones.

Jo-seph said, For sev-en years there will be no lack of food in the land, and all will go well; and then there will come a time of great want, and rich and poor will be in need of food, and not a few will starve to death.

PHA-RA-OH'S DREAM.

Let the king choose a wise man to see that corn is laid up in the land when the good years bring the rich growth, so that there will be no lack of food in the years when the crops are small.

And the king said to Jo-seph, Since God hath

showed thee all this there is none so wise as thou art. So he put him in charge of all the land of E-gypt, and he was to rank next to the king. And the king took a ring from his own hand and put it on Jo-seph's hand, and when he rode out, men bowed the knee, and his word was law in all the land. And Jo-seph took a wife, and he who was brought to E-gypt a slave, was now a rich man.

And there came years when the grain grew rank in the fields, and the crops were large. And Jo-seph saw that a large part of it was laid up, and that there was no waste of the good food. For the end of those rich years came and then there was a time of dearth in all the lands, when the earth would not yield, and men and beasts were in want of food.

But there was no lack of corn in E-gypt. And Jo-seph sold the corn that he had stored in the barns, and crowds came in to buy it.

When Ja-cob heard that corn could be bought in E-gypt, he told his sons to go down and buy some, that they might not starve to death.

And ten of them went down to buy corn in E-gypt. But Ja-cob kept Ben-ja-min at home, for fear he would be lost to him as Jo-seph was lost.

When Ja-cob's ten sons came to the place where Jo-seph was, they bowed down to the ground. And

JO-SEPH AND HIS BROTH-ERS.

Jo-seph knew them at once, but they did not know him, or give a thought to his dreams.

And Jo-seph spoke in a rough voice, and said, Whence come ye?

And they said, From the land of Ca-naan to buy food.

And he said, Ye are spies, and have come to see how poor the land is.

And they said to him, Nay, my lord, but to buy food are we come. We are all one man's sons; and we are true men, and not spies.

But Jo-seph would have it that they were spies.

And they said, There were twelve of us, sons of one man. Young Ben-ja-min is at home with his fa-ther, and one is dead.

And Jo-seph said, Go prove that ye are not spies; let one of the ten that are here go and fetch the young lad, Ben-ja-min. And he put them in jail for three days. And he said, Let one of you be bound, and kept in the guard-house, while the rest of you take back the corn that you need. And they said that they would do this.

Then he took Sim-e-on from their midst, and had him bound, and put in the guard-house.

And he sent word to his men to fill their sacks with corn, and to put back the price in each sack, and to give them food to eat on the way. And thus did Jo-seph do good to those who did ill to him.

When Ja-cob's nine sons went home they told all that had been said and done to them, and that the lord of the land bade them bring Ben-ja-min down to E-gypt or he would think they were spies, and their lives would not be safe.

Ja-cob said, My son shall not go down with you, for his broth-er is dead, and he is all I have left. If harm should come to him on the way, I should die of grief.

THE MEET-ING OF JO SEPH AND BEN-JA-MIN.

When the corn they had brought from E-gypt was all gone, Ja-cob told his sons to go down and buy more. And Ju-dah spoke up and said, The man swore we should not see his face if Ben-ja-min was not with us. If thou wilt send him with us we will go; but if thou wilt not send him we will not go down.

Then Ja-cob said, If it must be so, take Ben-ja-min with you, and may God give you grace with this man that he may send my two boys back to me.

So the men took Ben-ja-min and went down to E-gypt, and stood face to face with Jo-seph.

And they gave Jo-seph the gifts they had brought, and bowed down to the earth. And he asked how they all were, and if their fath-er was well; and when he saw Ben-ja-min he said, Is this the young broth-er of whom you spoke? And he said to the lad, God be good to thee, my son.

And Jo-seph's heart was so full at sight of the boy, and he longed so to throw his arms round him, that he had to make haste and leave the room that his tears might not be seen.

Then he came back and had the feast set out, and all did eat and drink, and were glad at heart. And when the time came for his guests to leave, Jo-seph told his head man to fill their sacks with corn, to put their gold back in the mouth of the sacks, and to put in the young lad's sack the cup from which Jo-seph drank at each meal.

Joseph and his Brethren.

This was done, and when they had gone out of the town Jo-seph bade his man go and say to them: My lord's cup is lost, and you must know who stole it.

And when the man came up with Ja-cob's sons, he said just what Jo-seph told him to say. And they were all in a rage, and said: Why does my lord say such things of us? If the cup is found on one of us, kill him; and make the rest of us slaves.

And each one of them cast his sack on the ground, and loosed it at the top. And the cup was found in Ben-ja-min's sack. Then they rent their clothes, and in great grief went back to Jo-seph's house and found him there. And they fell down at his feet.

And Ju-dah said, God has found out our sins.

JA-COB BLESS-ES JO-SEPH'S CHIL-DREN.

Let us be your slaves; and take him as well in whose sack the cup was found.

Jo-seph said, No; but the man in whose sack the cup was found shall stay and serve me, and the rest shall go in peace.

Then Ju-dah, who had sworn that he would bring back the boy, said to Jo-seph: If we go home, and our fath-er sees the lad is not with us, he will die of grief. For his life is bound up in the lad's life.

Jo-seph could not keep back his tears, and when he had sent all the men of E-gypt out of the room, he said to his broth-ers, Come near, I pray you.

And they came near. And he said, I am Jo-seph, whom ye sold in-to E-gypt. But grieve not that ye did this thing, for God did send me here that I might save your lives. Go home and tell my fath-er that God hath made me lord of all Egypt, and bid him come down to me at once. And say that he shall dwell near me, in the land of Go-shen, and I will take care of him.

Then he fell on Ben-ja-min's neck, and they wept; and he kissed his broth-ers and shed tears, but they were tears of joy.

Ja-cob took all that he had and went down to E-gypt. And three-score and ten souls went with him. And they dwelt in the land of Go-shen, and Ja-cob died there.

Jo-seph's breth-ren thought that he would hate them now that their fath-er was dead. And they fell down at his feet and wept and prayed that he would do them no harm

Jo-seph bade them fear not, for he would take care of them and be kind to them. They had meant to do him an ill turn when he was a lad, but God had made it turn out for good, and it was all right. And Jo-seph lived to a good old age, and had two sons, whose names were E-phra-im and Ma-nas-seh.

THROUGH THE RED SEA AND THE WILDERNESS

By and by there rose up a new King in E-gypt who knew not Jo-seph. He was called Pha-ra-oh, as this was the name by which all the kings of E-gypt were known. And he said there were more He-brews, or Jews, in the land than there ought to be, and if war should break out, and these Jews should take sides with the foes of Pha-ra-oh and his race, they would be sure to win. So he set them hard tasks, and made them bear great loads, and did all he could to vex them, and still they grew in strength. God had said they were to be as the stars in the sky, and as the sands of the sea, that no one could count. And the king of E-gypt tried to stop this thing.

And he made it a law that if a boy child was born to the He-brews it should be put to death at once; but a girl child might live. And this was the cause of great grief to the poor bond slaves, who were forced to do the will of the great king.

One day the prin-cess went down to bathe in the stream that ran near her house. And her maids went with her. And as she stood on the shore of the Nile, she caught sight of a small boat built like an ark, that was hid in the reeds, and sent her maids to fetch it out.

When the prin-cess looked in the ark she saw the child. And the babe wept. And the prin-cess tried to soothe it, but the child cried the more, for her voice was a strange one. And she said, This is a He-brew child.

And one of her maids spoke up, and said, Shall I get thee a He-brew nurse, that she may nurse the child for thee?

And the prin-cess said, Yes; go.

And the maid brought her own and the babe's moth-er, to whom the prin-cess said, Take this child and nurse it for me, and I will pay thee for it.

And the wo-man took the child and took care of it.

THE FIND-ING OF MO-SES.

And the child grew, and was brought down to Pha-ra-oh's house, and the prin-cess made him her son, and gave him the name of Mo-ses: which means "Drawn out."

One day, when Mo-ses had grown to be a man, he went out to look at those of his own race, and to watch them at their tasks. And while he stood there a man from E-gypt struck one of the Jews; and when Mo-ses looked to the right and to the left and saw that no one was near, he slew the one from E-gypt and hid him in the sand.

And the next day, when he went out, he saw there was a fight be-tween two He-brews. And he said to the one who was in the wrong, Why did you strike that man?

And he said, Who made thee our judge? Dost thou want to kill me, as thou didst the one from E-gypt?

And Mo-ses was scared, for he thought no one knew of this deed.

As soon as it came to the ears of the king, he sought to slay Mo-ses. But Mo-ses fled from him, and dwelt in the land of Mid-i-an, and found a wife there, and took care of the flocks of Jeth-ro, his wife's fath-er.

One day as he led his flock out in search of food he came to Mount Ho-reb, and there he saw a flame

MO-SES A-VENG-ES A MAL-TREAT-ED IS-RA-EL-ITE.

MO-SES CALLED TO LEAD IS-RA-EL OUT OF E-GYPT.

of fire stream out of a bush, and the bush was not burnt in the least.

As he drew near the bush the Lord spoke to him out of the flame, and Mo-ses hid his face, for he dared not look on God.

The Lord said, The cry of the chil-dren of Is-ra-el has come up to me, and I have seen how ill they have been used. And I will send thee to Pha-ra-oh that thou mayst bring them forth out of the land of E-gypt.

But Mo-ses was loth to go.

And the Lord said, What is that in thine hand? And Moses said, A rod, And the Lord said, Cast it on the ground. And he cast it on the ground, and it was changed to a snake, and Mo-ses fled from it. Then the Lord said to Mo-ses, Put forth thine hand, and take it by the tail. And Mo-ses did so, and it was a rod in his hand. And

MO-SES BROUGHT BE-FORE PHA-RA-OH'S DAUGH-TER.

the Lord said, Put now thy hand in on thy breast. And he put it in, and when he drew it out it was white, and like a dead hand. And he put his hand in once more, and drew it out, and it was like the rest of his flesh.

Then Mo-ses said, O, my Lord, I am not fit to do this work, for I am slow of speech, and a man of few words.

And the Lord said to him, I will be with thee, and teach thee what thou wilt say.

Still Mo-ses was loth to go, and the Lord was wroth with him, and said, Take Aa-ron with thee. He can speak well. And thou shalt tell him what to say and do, and I will teach you, and with this rod in thy hand thou shalt do great things, as if thou wert God.

So Mo-ses took his wife and his sons and put them on an ass, and went back to E-gypt with the rod of God in his hand.

And Mo-ses and Aa-ron went in to the king and begged him to let the He-brews go out of the land. And he would not, but laid more work on the men, and bade them make bricks with-out straw, and do all sorts of hard tasks.

And the Lord sent plagues on the land, and the ponds dried up, and all the large streams were turned to blood, and the fish died, and the stench of them made the air scarce fit to breathe. And there was no wa-ter they could drink. Then there came a plague of frogs, and they were so thick in the land that Pha-ra-oh said he would let the chil-dren of Is-ra-el go if Mo-ses would rid him of the frogs at the same time.

But the king did not keep his word, for as soon as he found the frogs grew less, he said the He-brews should not go.

MOS-ES AT THE BURN-ING BUSH.

Then the Lord smote the land with lice; but still Pha-ra-oh's heart was hard.

Then the Lord sent flies in such swarms that

there was no place that was free from them, and they made the food not fit to eat.

And the king told Mo-ses he would let the bond-slaves go to serve their God, but they were not to go far till the land was rid of flies. Then Mo-ses went forth and prayed to God, and the flies left the land. But still the king's heart was hard, and he would not let them go.

Then the Lord sent worse plagues: the flocks and herds died; there were boils on man and beast; the crops did not come up, and rain, hail, and balls of fire came down from the sky. And still the heart of the king was as hard as stone. Then the Lord sent lo-custs, that ate up all the hail had left, and there was not a green leaf on the trees nor a blade of grass to be seen in the whole land.

And the king bade Mo-ses to set him free from this plague. And the Lord sent a strong west wind, that blew the flies in-to the Red Sea. Yet Pha-ra-oh would not let the He-brews go.

Then the Lord told Mo-ses to stretch out his hand, and there came up a thick cloud that made the land so dark that the folks staid in bed for three days. And Pha-ra-oh said to Mo-ses, Get thee out of my sight. For if I see thy face thou shalt die.

And Mo-ses said, Thou hast well said: I will see thy face no more.

Through the Red Sea and the Wilderness.

And the Lord sent one more plague on E-gypt: he smote the first-born of men and of beasts, and a great cry was heard through the land. And then Pha-ra-oh had to let the chil-dren of Is-ra-el go, for he could not keep up this strife with God. And Mo-ses led the He-brew chil-dren out of E-gypt, and the Lord sent a cloud by day and a fire by night to show them the way.

And when they were in camp by the Red Sea, they looked up and saw Pha-ra-oh and his hosts, and were in great fear lest he should kill them. And they cried out to the Lord, and blamed Mo-ses that he had brought them in-to such straits.

MIR-IAM, THE SIS-TER OF MO-SES, AND THE WO-MEN OF IS-RAEL SING-ING PRAISES.

As they came to the Red Sea, Mo-ses raised his rod and the sea rose like a wall on each side, and the chil-dren of Is-ra-el went on dry land through the midst of the sea.

Then Pha-ra-oh and his hosts came close in the rear, and passed down be-tween the great sea-wall that rose at the right hand and at the left. And the waves that had stood still at a sign from God were let loose, and the king and his horse-men were swept out of sight.

When the chil-dren of Is-ra-el came out of the Red Sea they were three days with naught to drink. And when they came to a stream, called Ma-rah, they found it bitter. And they said to Mo-ses, What shall we drink?

And Mo-ses cried out to the Lord, and the Lord showed him a tree, and when he had cast a branch of it in the stream it was made sweet at once. And they came to E-lim, where were ten wells and three-score palm-trees, and there they made their camp.

It was not long ere there was a great cry for bread.

And Mo-ses plead with God, and when the sun went down that day quails flew in-to the camp, and they had all the meat they cared to eat. At dawn of the next day, as soon as the dew was off the ground, there came a rain of what was at first thought to be hail-stones.

But Mo-ses said it was food that God had sent

RESCUE OF THE IS-RA-EL-ITES AND DE-STRUC-TION OF THE E-GYP-TIANS IN THE RED SEA.

them to eat, and they were to take all and no more than they would need for one day. For they were to trust in God that he would feed them each day. On the sixth day they were to take what would last them for two days, for no food fell on the day of rest.

This new food was called man-na.

As they went on they came to Reph-i-dim, but found no wa-ter to drink. And they found fault with Mo-ses. And Mo-ses cried out, Lord, what shall I do to these, who have a mind to stone me?

At this time they were near Mount Ho-reb, where God spoke to Mo-ses out of a bush that was on fire, yet not burnt.

And God told Mo-ses to take his rod in his hand and go on till he came to a rock. And this rock he was to strike with his rod, and wa-ter would flow out of it. And Mo-ses did as the Lord told him, and when he struck the rock the wa-ter ran out.

In the third month from the time they left E-gypt, the chil-dren of Is-ra-el came near Mount Si-na-i, and went in-to camp. And Mo-ses went up to the top of the Mount, and the Lord spoke to him there.

On the third day a thick cloud of smoke rose from Mount Si-na-i, and a loud noise that made those that heard it quake with fear. And Mo-ses led his flock out of the camp, and they came and stood at the foot of the mount. And they said to

MOSES BREAKETH THE TABLES.

THROUGH MO-SES THE LORD PUN-ISH-ES IS-RA-EL'S I-DOL-A-TRY.

Mo-ses, Speak thou with us, and we will hear; but let not God speak with us lest we die. But Mo-ses told them that God had not come to make them die, but to make them fear to do aught that did not please him.

And God gave to Mo-ses two blocks of stone on which were the Ten Laws that the chil-dren of Is-ra-el were to keep.

Now while Mo-ses was in the mount, face to face with God, those whom he had brought out of E-gypt were in camp at the foot. And Mo-ses staid so long that they made up their minds he would not come back. So they said to Aa-ron, Make us a God that we can bow down to. And Aa-ron bade them throw all the gold they had into the fire. And they did so, and it took the form of a calf. And when God saw this he was not pleased, but bade Mo-ses make haste down the mount.

When Mo-ses came down from the mount with the two flat stones in his hands, and drew near the camp, and saw what had been done, he was in a great rage. He cast the blocks of stone out of his hands and broke them at the foot of the mount.

Then he took the calf which they had made, and burnt it in the fire till there was nought left of it but a fine dust. And Mo-ses begged God to blot out the sins of those whom he had led out of E-gypt.

And the Lord told Mo-ses to hew out two blocks of stone like to the first, and bring them up with him to the top of Mount Si-na-i.

This Mo-ses did, and the Lord wrote on them the Ten Laws that all were to keep if they would reach the land they sought.

They were more than two-score years on the road, and in that time they met with plagues, and there was strife in their midst, yet as they went there was the fire by night and the cloud by day to show that the Lord was with them.

When they came to Mount Hor and were yet a long way from Ca-naan, Aa-ron died, and there was great grief at his loss. They were sick at heart and foot-sore, and spoke hard words of God and Mo-ses. There is no bread here for us, they said, and no wa-ter, and we loathe this man-na. And for this sin God sent snakes in-to their camp, and they bit the chil-dren of Is-ra-el so that a few of them died. Then they plead with Mo-ses to rid them of the snakes, and make their peace with God.

And Mo-ses prayed for them. And God told him to make a snake like to those which bit his flock, and set it up on a pole. And all those who would look at this brass snake should be made well.

And Mo-ses did so. And this sign was meant

to show forth Christ, who was to heal men of their sins, and to be raised up on a cross.

And Mo-ses led his flock till they came to the plains of Mo-ab. And Ba-lak, the king of that land, thought they had come to fight with him, and he sent a man named Ba-laam out to curse them and drive them back. He told Ba-laam he would make him a rich man if he would do this thing, and as Ba-laam was fond of wealth

BA-LAAM AND THE ASS.

he said he would do the the king's will. So he set forth on his ass, and had not gone far when he met an an-gel with a drawn sword in his hand. Ba-laam did not see him, but the ass did and turned out of the road. But the an-gel went on and stood in a place where there was a wall on each side.

When the ass came to the place she went close to the wall and tried to get by. But she hurt Ba-laam's foot and he struck her and made her go on. And the an-gel went on and stood in a place where there was no room to turn to the right hand or the left.

Then the ass shook with fright and fell down on the ground. And Ba-laam struck her with the staff that he had in his hand.

And the Lord made the ass speak like a man, and say, What have I done to thee that thou hast struck me these three times?

Ba-laam said, To make thee move on: I would there were a sword in my hand, for I would kill thee.

Then the ass said, Am I not thine? and have I been wont to do so to thee? And Ba-laam said, No. Then the Lord made Ba-laam see the an-gel that stood in the way with a drawn sword in his hand, and Ba-laam bowed his face to the ground.

Then the an-gel said, Why hast thou struck thine ass these three times? Lo, I came out to stop thee, and to turn thee from the way of sin. And the ass saw me, and turned from the path, and if she had not done so I would have slain thee.

Through the Red Sea and the Wilderness.

Then he said to Ba-laam, Go with the men the king has sent, but say on-ly what I shall tell thee.

So Ba-laam went with the men, and when Ba-lak heard that he was come he went out to meet him. The next day Ba-lak took Ba-laam to a high place, from whence he could look down on the camp of Is-ra-el, and curse them.

But the Lord would not let him curse them, but made him speak good things of them. This was done on three high mounts, and at last the king was wroth, and said to Ba-laam, I sent for thee to curse my foes, and lo, these three times hast thou blest them.

And Ba-lak bade him make haste and go back

MO-SES ON MOUNT NE-BO.

to his own home. And Ba-laam went off as poor as he came, for Ba-lak gave him none of his gold.

The Lord brought Mo-ses and his flock to the banks of the Jor-dan, which they would have to cross to reach the land of Ca-naan. And while they were there, Mo-ses went up to the top of Mount Ne-bo to talk with God. And God told him how large the land was that he would give to the chil-dren of Is-ra-el. And he said that Mo-ses should look on it, but should not step foot in the land. And Mo-ses died on Mount Ne-bo, and though an old man, was well and strong till the Lord took him. And no one knows in what part of the earth his grave was made.

HOW JOSHUA AND JEPHTHAH FOUGHT FOR THE LORD

When Mo-ses died, Josh-u-a took charge of the chil-dren of Is-ra-el, and sought to do God's will, as Mo-ses had done. And Josh-u-a sent word through the camp that in three days they would cross the Jor-dan. And when they set foot in the stream the waves stood back as they did in the Red Sea, and they went through Jor-dan on dry ground. And as they came up out of the stream the waves closed up and there was no path-way through them.

The chil-dren of Is-ra-el made their camp at a place called Gil-gal; and as there was no lack of food in this good land, the Lord ceased to rain down man-na for them to eat.

The next day Josh-u-a left the camp and came near to the walls of Jer-i-cho. There he met a man with a drawn sword in his hand. And Josh-u-a said, Art thou for us or for our foes?

And the man said, As prince of the Lord's host am

PASS-ING THROUGH THE JOR-DAN.

I now come. And at these words Josh-u-a fell on his face to the earth; for he knew it was the Lord that spoke to him.

The Lord told Josh-u-a to have no fear of the

king of Jer-i-cho, for the chil-dren of Is-ra-el should take the town. All their men of war were to march round the town once each day for six days. Some of the priests were to bear the ark, which held the things they made use of when they went in to talk with God, and some were to blow on rams' horns.

And the next day—when the six days were at an end—they were to march round the town sev-en times, and the priests were to blow their horns. And when the men of Is-ra-el heard a long loud blast they were all to give a great shout and the wall would fall flat to the ground, and they could march in and take the town.

Josh-u-a bade his men do all the Lord had said; and told them to make no noise with their voice as they went their rounds till he bade them shout. And when the priests blew their horns for the last time, Josh-u-a cried, Shout! for the Lord is with us! and there was a great shout and the wall fell, and they took the town; and the fame of Josh-u-a spread through all the lands.

Josh-u-a fought with more than a score of kings and won their lands from them; but yet there was much land in Ca-naan for which the chil-dren of Is-ra-el would have to fight.

But as the years went on, Josh-u-a grew so old that he could not lead his men to war as he used to

How Joshua and Jephthah Fought for the Lord.

do. And he called his flock to him and told them how good the Lord had been to them. And he bade them love the Lord and serve him, and put from

JER-I-CHO CON-QUERED AND DE-STROYED.

them all strange gods. He said, Choose ye this day whom ye will serve; but as for me and my house we will serve the Lord.

And the men said, The Lord hath done great

things for us, and him will we serve, for he is our God.

And Josh-u-a took a great stone and set it up neath an oak tree that stood near where the ark was kept at Shi-loh. And this stone, he said, was to be a sign of the vow they had made there to serve the Lord. And when the talk was at an end, the men went to their own homes.

And ere long Josh-u-a died. And they laid him in the part of the land that God gave him as his own, on the north side of the hill of Ga-ash.

Then the chil-dren of Is-ra-el went to war with the tribes that were in the land of Ca-naan, as Josh-u-a had told them to do. But they did not drive them all out, as they should have done, but made friends with those that were left, and were led in-to sin, and were made to serve as bond-slaves. And when they were sick of their sins, and sought the help of the Lord, he sent men to rule them, and to lead them out to war and set them free from these friends who proved to be the worst kind of foes.

Now there was a man in Is-ra-el whose name was Jeph-thah. He was a brave man, and had done great deeds, but the chil-dren of Is-ra-el were not kind to him, so he fled from their land, and went to live in the land of Tob. But when the Jews had need of a man to lead them out to war, they thought

How Joshua and Jephthah Fought for the Lord.

of Jeph-thah. And they said, Come, and be at the head of us when we go out to fight the Am-mon-ites.

And Jeph-thah said, If I go with you, and win the fight, will you make me judge in Is-ra-el?

And they said they would.

Now ere the fight took place, Jeph-thah made a vow that if the Lord would let him win he would give to God — that is, would slay and burn as if it were a lamb — the first who came out of his doors to meet him when he went back to his home.

Jeph-thah should not have made this rash vow, and need not have kept it if he had asked God to for-give the sin.

JEPH-THAH AND HIS DAUGH-TER

He went out to fight the Am-mon-ites, and by the help of the Lord the chil-dren of Is-ra-el were set free from them.

When the fight was at an end Jeph-thah went back to his home, and the first to come out to meet him was his own child, a fair young maid, whose face was bright with joy. She was all the child that Jeph-thah had, and when he saw her he rent his clothes and told her of the vow he had made.

And she said, My fath-er, if thou hast made a vow to the Lord, do with me as thou hast said. And he took his child and did to her as he had said he would, and all the young girls in Is-ra-el wept for her.

Jeph-thah was a judge for six years, and then he died.

SAMSON: THE STRONG MAN

The Jews kept on in their sins, and took no pains to please the Lord, and so fell in-to the hands of the Phil-is-tines.

And there was at that time a man in Is-ra-el whose name was Ma-no-ah. Both he and his wife served the Lord; and they had no child. And God sent one of his an-gels to the wife of Ma-no-ah to tell

JEPHTHAH AND HIS DAUGHTER.

SAMSON KILLS A LION.

Samson: the Strong Man.

her that she should have a son who was to be brought up to serve the Lord, and to do his work.

Ere long Ma-no-ah and his wife had a son, to whom they gave the name of Sam-son.

And the child grew, and the Lord blest him. And when he was grown up he went to Tin-muth, where he met a Phil-is-tine wo-man and fell in love with her.

Then his pa-rents plead with him to find a wife in Is-ra-el, and not to take this one who was no friend to his race. But Sam-son would not give her up.

So they went with him to Tin-muth. And on the way a li-on ran out and roared at him. And Sam-son put his arms round the beast and tore him with his hands as if he had been a young kid. But he did not tell his fath-er and moth-er what he had done.

The time soon came when Sam-son was to set the Jews free from the Phil-is-tines. And he went down to one of their towns and slew a few of their men, and then went back to his own home, while his wife stayed in Tin-muth.

When it was time to bring the wheat in from the field, Sam-son went down to see his wife, and took with him a young kid. But when he came to the house her fath-er would not let him go in, and told him that she was his wife no more, but had gone to live with some one else. Then Sam-son was in a great rage, and he went and caught more than ten score fox-es, and set bits of wood on fire, and tied these fire-brands to their tails, and let them loose in the fields and vine-yards of the Phil-is-tines.

And they set fire to the grain, and burnt it all up.

And the grape-vines and fruit trees were burnt, and much harm was done.

When the Phil-is-tines found out that it was Sam-son who had done this they took his wife and her fath-er and burnt them to death. And Sam-son fought and slew a host of the Phil-is-tines, and then went on the top of a high rock called E-tam to stay there.

Then a crowd of men went up with a rush to the top of the rock, and they said to Sam-son, We have come to bind thee, that we may give thee into the hands of the Phil-is-tines.

Sam-son made them swear that they would not put him to death, and they bound him with strong cords and brought him down from the rock.

As they drew near the camp of the Phil-is-tines a great shout went up from the men there. And the Lord gave Sam-son such strength that he broke the cords from his arms as if they had been burnt threads.

And Sam-son took up the jaw-bone of an ass,

Samson: the Strong Man.

and with it he fought the Phil-is-tines and slew a host of them.

Then a great thirst came on him, and there was no well near from which he could drink. And he grew so weak that he cried out to the Lord not to let him die of thirst or fall into the hands of his foes.

And the Lord made a spring at that place and water ran out, and when Sam-son had drunk, his strength came back to him.

Sam-son came to the town of Ga-za, and went in a house there. Now the Phil-is-tines dwelt in Ga-za, and when they heard that Sam-son was there they shut the gates of the town, and kept watch near them all night. They said when the day dawns we will kill him.

SAM-SON SLAY-ING THE PHIL-IS-TINES.

But in the dead of the night Sam-son rose up and came to the gates of the town, and when he found them shut he took them up—posts, bar and all—and bore them a long way off to the top of a hill.

Sam-son's hair had not been cut, and it had grown thick and long. And there was a wo-man named De-li-lah whom Sam-son used to go and see. And when the Phil-is-tines heard of it they came to her and told her if she would find out how they might bind Sam-son and bear him off, they would give her a large sum of gold.

So when Sam-son came to De-li-lah's house she said to him, Tell me, I pray thee what makes thee so strong, and with what thou couldst be bound and not break loose?

Sam-son said if they bound him with seven green withes—that is, cords made out of soft twigs—he would be so weak that he could not break them.

When De-li-lah told this to the Phil-is-tines they brought her seven green withes, and Sam-son let her bind him with them. Now she had men hid in her house who were to take Sam-son if he could not break the twigs. And when she had bound him she cried out, The Phil-is-tines seize thee, Sam-son! And as soon as she had said these words he broke the green withes as if they were burnt threads.

Then De-li-lah knew that Sam-son made fun of

her and told her lies, and she said once more, Tell me, I pray thee, with what thou canst be bound and not break loose.

Sam-son told her if he were bound with new

SAM-SON'S DOWN-FALL.

ropes, which had not been used, that his strength would leave him, and he would be too weak to break them.

So she took new ropes and bound him. But ere the men who were hid in the room could spring out and take him, Sam-son broke the ropes from his arms as if they had been threads.

Then De-li-lah told Sam-son that he did but mock her and tell her lies, and she begged him to let her know how he might be bound.

And he said if she would weave his hair with the web in the loom his strength would go from him. And she wove his long hair in with the web, and made it fast with a large peg that was part of the loom.

Then she cried out, and Sam-son rose up and went off with the great peg, and the whole of the web that was in the loom.

Then she said he did not love her or he would not make sport of her in this way. And she teased him each day, and gave him no peace, so that at last he had to tell her the truth.

He said his hair had not been cut since he was born, and if it were shaved off he would lose all his strength.

It was wrong for Sam-son to tell her this, for she was bad at heart and not a true friend. But he did not know then how great was his sin.

De-li-lah knew that this time Sam-son had told her the truth; so she sent for the Phil-is-tines to come up to her house.

Then while Sam-son slept, she had a man come

in and shave all the hair from his head. And when this was done she cried out, The Phil-is-tines seize thee, Sam-son.

And he woke from his sleep, and knew not his strength had gone from him.

Then the Phil-is-tines took him and put out his eyes, brought him down to Ga-za, and bound him with chains of brass. And they made him fast to a millstone, and he had to work hard to grind their corn.

SAM-SON AND DE-LI-LAH.

While he was shut up in jail Sam-son had time to think of his sins, and he no doubt cried out to the

Lord to keep him. For his hair grew out and his strength came back. But the Phil-is-tines did not know this.

They had made their own god, and its name was Da-gon. And they thought that Da-gon gave Sam-son in-to their hands, and loud was their praise of him. And all the Phil-is-tines met in the large house that had been built for Da-gon that they might bow down to their god and give him thanks.

The crowd was great, and their hearts were full of joy. And they said, Send for Sam-son that he may make sport for us. And poor blind Sam-son was brought in, and sat down in their midst. And those in the house and those on the roof made sport of him in all sorts of ways.

And Sam-son put his arms round two of the great posts that held up the house. And he bent down, and the house fell, and most of the Phil-is-tines were killed. Sam-son died with them, and by his death slew more of the foes of Is-ra-el than he had slain in all his life.

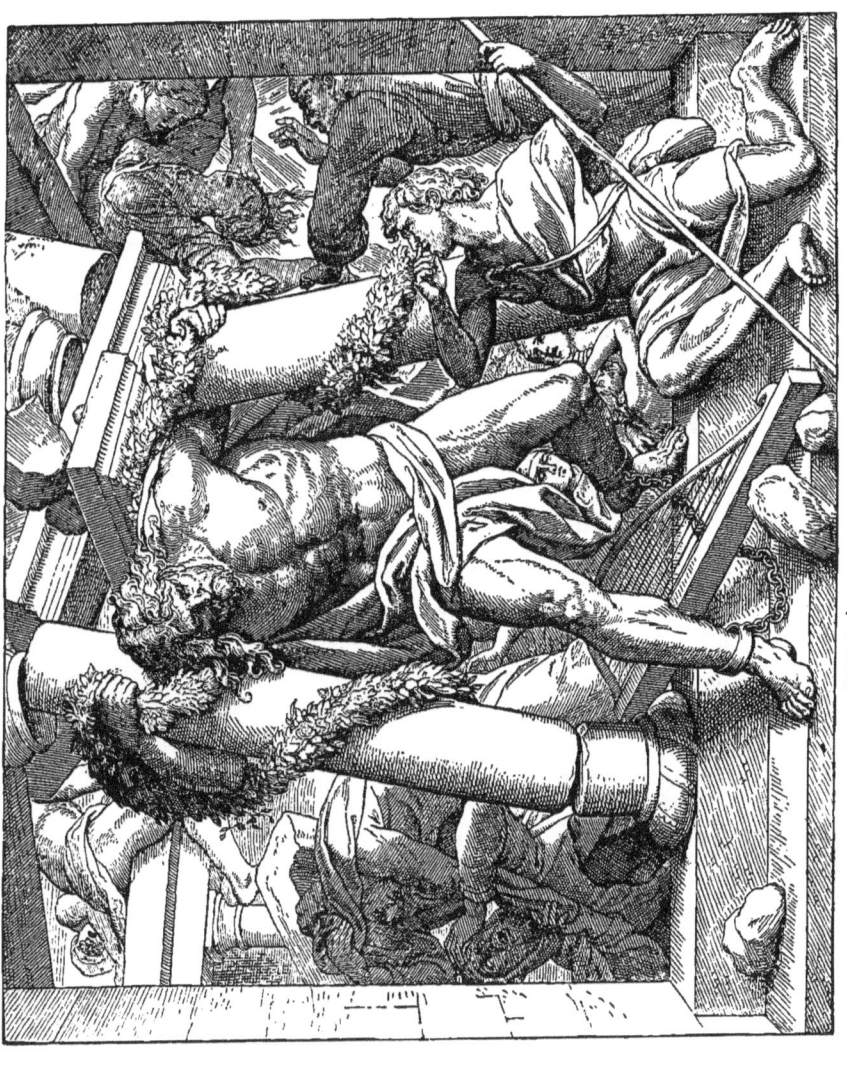

SAMSON'S VENGEANCE AND DEATH.

THE WERNER COMPANY'S PUBLICATIONS.

REMINGTON'S FRONTIER SKETCHES.

By FREDERIC REMINGTON. A beautiful new pictorial, dainty in all its appointments, of highest artistic excellence. This choice collection comprises many of Remington's most notable drawings, displaying to splendid advantage his great talents and peculiar genius. 9½x13 inches. Japanese vellum binding, gilt edged, boxed. **$2.00.**

THE DETERMINATION OF SEX.

Schenk's Theory. By LEOPOLD SCHENK, M. D., Prof. of Embryology in the Royal and Imperial University at Vienna, and Pres. of the Austrian Embryological Institute. The last and greatest physiological discovery of the age. 12mo. Artistic cloth binding. **$1.50.**

THE STORY OF AMERICA.

The latest and best Young People's History of the United States. By HEZEKIAH BUTTERWORTH, for many years editor of the *Youth's Companion*, author of "Zig Zag Journeys," "The Knight of Liberty," "In the Boyhood of Lincoln," etc., etc. 8vo. 850 pages. **$1.50.**

SPAIN IN HISTORY.

From the days of the Visigoths, 350 A. D. to the present hour. By Prof. JAS. A. HARRISON, Prof. of History and Modern Languages at Washington and Lee University. Revised and brought down to date by G. MERCER ADAM. Large 12mo. Profusely illustrated. Emblematic buckram binding. **$1.50.**

CONQUERING THE WILDERNESS.

Or Heroes and Heroines of Pioneer Life and Adventure. By Col. FRANK TRIPLETT. **$1.50.**

BOYS OF THE BIBLE.

A book for boys of America. By THOS. W. HANDFORD. Mr. Handford gives a most reverent and interesting account of the youth of our Saviour. The story is one that cannot fail to inspire respect. **$1.00.**

THE FARMER'S ENCYCLOPEDIA.

Embracing articles on the horse, the farm, health, cattle, sheep, swine, poultry, bees, the dog, toilet, social life, etc. Size 8x5½ inches; 636 pages; green cloth binding. Price, **$1.50.**

FOREST AND JUNGLE.

An account of the last African expedition sent out. By P. T. BARNUM. The latest and greatest illustrated history of the animal kingdom, capture and training of wild beasts, birds and reptiles. Thrilling adventures in all quarters of the globe. Written in easy instructive form for boys and girls. 8vo., 502 pages, 84 chapters, hundreds of illustrations, large, clear type. Cloth, scarlet, stamped in black and silver. **$1.50.**

HOME OCCUPATIONS FOR LITTLE CHILDREN.

By KATHERINE BEEBE. What Miss Beebe's "First School Year" is to the primary teacher this little volume is intended to be to mothers. Miss Beebe believes that the ceaseless activity of children calls for employment, and "Home Occupations" is full of ways and means for mothers. Enthusiastically endorsed by the press and leading kindergartners. **75 cents.**

THE PILGRIM'S PROGRESS.

New edition. Printed from new plates. Extra quality, super-calendered paper. Copiously illustrated. The most attractive Pilgrim's Progress on the market. 200 illustrations. Large quarto, 400 pages, **$1.50.**

For sale by all booksellers, or sent postpaid on receipt of the advertised price.

THE WERNER COMPANY, Publishers. - Akron, O.

THE WERNER COMPANY'S PUBLICATIONS.

THE WHITE HOUSE COOK BOOK.
By Hugo Ziemann, steward of the White House, and Mrs. F. L. Gillette. New and enlarged edition. $1.25.

NAPOLEON FROM CORSICA TO ST. HELENA.
De Luxe Edition. Especial attention is invited to this new and beautiful pictorial. It embodies a bird's-eye view of the life and career of Napoleon the Great. The numerous beautiful colored plates were made especially for it in France. The rich binding of royal purple, embossed in gold and white enamel, is in harmony with the other elegant appointments. Each copy is securely boxed. $4.00.

DEEDS OF DARING BY THE AMERICAN SOLDIER.
Thrilling narratives of personal daring in both armies during the Civil War. $1.50.

ILLUSTRATED HOME BOOK—WORLD'S GREAT NATIONS.
Large quarto volume. 670 pages. Scenes, events, manners and customs of many nations, with over 1,000 engravings by the most eminent artists. Present edition just published. Silk cloth, gold-stamped binding, calendered paper. $1.50.

OUR BUSINESS BOYS; OR, SECRETS OF SUCCESS.
By Rev. Francis E. Clark, Father of the Christian Endeavor movement. Small 12mo, pebble grain, 25 cents.

" Go-at-it-ive-ness is the first condition of success. Stick-to-it-ive-ness is the second."
" If a man would succeed, there must be continuity of work."
" I have never known dishonesty successful in the long run."
" The wish for *genteel occupation* is ruinous."
" Too many young men seek soft places, and go behind the counter, when they ought to go into the field or machine shop."

MASTERS OF BRUSH AND CHISEL.
A superb selection from the world's greatest galleries and most famous private collections. Price, $1.00.

THE CROWN JEWELS OF ART.
Painting and Sculpture. Masterpieces of artists and sculptors of all nationalities. Including all that is choicest from the World's Columbian Exhibit, the International London, Paris, Vienna, and Philadelphia Expositions. Price, $1.00.

HISTORIC MEN AND SCENES.
Portrayed by the Masters. A magnificent selection of most interesting pictures. Collected from all lands. Price, $1.00.

THE OLD MASTERS WITH THE CHILDREN.
Famous works of the world's greatest artists on juvenile subjects. Before the Judge, Cornelia and Her Jewels, Both Astonished, Crimean Gypsy Girl, Caught, Cut Finger, Christmas Box, Defiance, etc., etc. Price, $1.00.

EVERY DAY FACTS.
A complete single volume Cyclopedia for the American home. Fully up-to-date. Every Day Facts contains more than 1,000,000 facts, figures, and fancies, drawn from every land and language, and carefully classified for ready reference of teachers, students, business men, and the family circle. 483 pages; handsomely bound in paper. Price, 50 cents.

For sale by all booksellers, or sent postpaid on receipt of the advertised price.

THE WERNER COMPANY, Publishers, - Akron, O.

THE WERNER COMPANY'S PUBLICATIONS.

THE STORY OF CUBA.

From first to last. By MURAT HALSTEAD, veteran journalist, distinguished war correspondent, brilliant writer; for many years the friend and associate of the "Makers of History" of the Western World. There is no more graphic, incisive writer than he; no shrewder observer of men and events; no one who foretells more unerringly the trend of affairs, their sequence and conclusion. Cuba's struggles for liberty. Cause, crisis and destiny. Elegant silk-finished cloth, emblematic, ink and gold design, plain edges, $2.00; half morocco, corners tipped, gold back and center stamp, marbled edges, $2.75.

GERMANIA.

Two thousand years of German life. By JOHANNES SCHERR. Three hundred engravings. Text in German only. This famous work by the ablest of modern German historians, is a graphic narrative of the origin and grand career of the German people, a history of their religious, social, and domestic life; their development in literature, science, music, and art, and their advancement in military and political power to their present position as arbiters of the destiny of Europe. Cloth binding, ornamented in black and silver. Price, $1.00.

THE PRESIDENTIAL COOK BOOK.

The best household compendium published. Has a reputation that is national. It is based on its real worth. Every recipe it contains was actually tested by the authors and found to be invariably successful. Thoroughly up-to-date; large type; large pages plainly indexed. A handy volume. In brief, a perfect cook book. Price, 50 cents.

JOHN SHERMAN'S RECOLLECTIONS OF FORTY YEARS IN THE HOUSE, SENATE AND CABINET.

An autobiography. Being the personal reminiscences of the author, including the political and financial history of the United States during his public career. The Library Edition is issued in two royal octavo volumes containing over 1,200 pages, bound in the following styles:

Fine English Cloth, gold side and back stamps, plain edges, $7.50 per set.
Full sheep, library style, marbled edges, $10.00 per set.
Half morocco, gold center back, gilt edges, $12.00 per set.
Full Turkey morocco, antique, gilt edges, $16.00 per set.
Autograph edition, limited to one thousand numbered copies, printed on specially made paper, bound in three-quarters calf, gilt top and rough edges, imperial 8vo., boxed, $25.00 per set.

The household edition is issued in one royal octavo volume, containing about 950 pages, printed from new electrotype plates on superfine book paper, richly illustrated with carefully selected views, including places and scenes relating to the author's boyhood; also many portraits of his contemporaries in the Cabinet and Senate. In addition there are a large number of fac simile reproductions of letters from presidents, senators, governors, and well-known private citizens.

Half morocco, gold center back, marbled edges, $6.00.
Cloth, gold side and back stamp, $4.00.

MILITARY CAREER OF NAPOLEON THE GREAT.

By MONTGOMERY B. GIBBS. Not a technical military history, but a gossipy, anecdotal account of the career of Napoleon Bonaparte as his marshals and generals knew him on the battlefield and around the camp-fire. Crown, 8vo., with 32 full page illustrations. Nearly 600 pages; half green leather; gilt top and back; English laid paper; uncut edges. Price, $1.25.

For sale by all booksellers, or sent postpaid on receipt of the advertised price.

THE WERNER COMPANY, Publishers, - Akron, O.

THE WERNER COMPANY'S PUBLICATIONS.

THE GERMAN-ENGLISH BUSINESS LETTER WRITER.

A practical aid. Carefully prepared by competent hands, to assist in the transaction of business in either German or English. Any German with a slight knowledge of English can, with the assistance of this book, write an intelligent English business letter. The reverse is equally true. The young man fitting himself for a position requiring a practical knowledge of both German and English will find no simpler or more reliable help. Price, 35 cents.

THE QUEEN'S REIGN.

By Sir WALTER BESANT. Price, $2.50.

THE TEMPERANCE COOK BOOK.

Free from reference to ardent spirits. Over 1,100 tested recipes. Articles on carving, dinner giving, on serving, cooking for the sick, table etiquette. Good living and good health both considered. 440 pages, extra quality paper, clear type. Price, 50 cents.

GERMANY'S IRON CHANCELLOR.

By BRUNO GARLEPP. Translated from the German by SIDNEY WHITMAN, F. R. G. S., author of "Imperial Germany," "The Realm of the Hapsburgs," "Teutonic Studies," etc. The styles of binding and prices are as follows:

Fine vellum cloth, emblematic gold stamp, red edges, 475 pages, $8.00.
Half morocco, gold stamped, 475 pages, $10.00.
Full morocco, gold side and back stamps, gilt edges, 475 pages, $12.00.

THE WERNER UNIVERSAL EDUCATOR.

A manual of self-instruction in all branches of popular education. A complete cyclopedia of reference, in history, science, business, and literature. An imperial volume, 10½ inches long, 9 inches wide, and contains 830 double column pages; also one million facts and figures, one thousand forms and rules, five hundred illustrations, one hundred colored plates and diagrams, and sixty colored maps, all down to date. Half seal. Price, $5.50. Cloth, $4.00.

STREET TYPES OF GREAT CITIES.

By SIGMUND KRAUSZ. The queer people that you sometimes see as you wend your way through the crowded thoroughfares of a great city. The author has largely caught them with his camera, and we have before us snap shots, true to life, of all sorts and conditions of men. Price, $1.00.

STEAM, STEEL AND ELECTRICITY.

By JAS. W. STEELE. A new book which ought to be in every household in the country where there are young people, or their elders, who take an interest in the progress of the age. The book tells in plain, clear language the story of steam, of the age of steel, and the story of electricity. An up-to-date non-technical work for the general reader. Scientific in its facts, it is interesting as a novel. Illustrated by many pictures and diagrams. 12mo., half Russia. Price, $1.00.

MANUAL OF USEFUL INFORMATION.

A pocket encyclopedia. A world of knowledge. Embracing more than 1,000,000 facts, figures, and fancies, drawn from every land and language, and carefully classified for the ready reference of teachers, students, business men, and the family circle. Compiled by a score of editors under the direction of Mr. J. C. THOMAS, with an introduction by Frank A. Fitzpatrick, superintendent of city schools, Omaha, Neb. Full Morocco, gilt. Price, $3.00.

For sale by all booksellers, or sent postpaid on receipt of the advertised price.

THE WERNER COMPANY, Publishers, - Akron, O.

THE WERNER COMPANY'S PUBLICATIONS.

SCENIC AMERICA.

Or the Beauties of the Western Hemisphere. 256 half-tone pictures, with descriptions by JOHN L. STODDARD. Size, 11x14 inches, 128 pages. Bound in cloth with handsome side stamp. Price, **75 cents**.

PERSONAL RECOLLECTIONS OF GENERAL NELSON A. MILES.

The wonderful career of a self-made man. How he rose from a Second Lieutenant to the rank of Commander in Chief of the United States Army. Embracing the thrilling story of his famous Indian campaigns. In this volume the reader is brought face to face with the great Indian leaders: Geronimo, Crazy Horse, Sitting Bull, Chief Joseph, Lame Deer, etc. One of the most remarkable books of the century. A massive volume of 600 pages, printed on fine super-calendered paper, with nearly 200 superb engravings. Illustrated by FREDERIC REMINGTON and other eminent artists. Every page bristles with interest. An ever-changing panorama. A history in itself, distinctive, thrilling and well nigh incredible. Artistic cloth, chaste and elegant design, plain edges, **$4.00**.

THE THEORY AND PRACTICE OF TEACHING.

Presents the complete writings of DAVID P. PAGE, edited by Supt. J. M. GREENWOOD, of the Kansas City Schools, assisted by Prof. CYRUS W. HODGIN, of Earlham College, Ind. This new, revised and enlarged edition of this marvelously popular work contains a fresh and exceedingly interesting life of its noted author, with portrait. 12mo., 343 pages, cloth binding. Price, **$1.50**.

THE TEACHER IN LITERATURE.

Revised edition, is a publication of exceptional merit, containing selections from Ascham, Rousseau, Shenstone, Pestalozzi, Cowper, Goethe, Irving, Mitford, Bronte, Thackeray, Dickens, and others who have written on subjects pertaining to educational work from the Elizabethan period down. To this edition Dr. B. A. Hindsdale, Professor of Pedagogy, University of Michigan, has added an exhaustive paper on the history of the schoolmaster from earliest times as he appears in literature. 12mo. 447 pages. Price, **$1.50**.

MAGNER'S STANDARD HORSE AND STOCK BOOK.

A complete pictorial encyclopedia of practical reference for horse and stock owners. By D. MAGNER, author of the Art of Taming and Training Horses, assisted by twelve leading veterinary surgeons. Comprising over 1,200 pages. Containing over 1,750 illustrations. The finest and most valuable farmer's book in the world. Cloth binding, **$4.00**; half Russia, **$5.50**.

MARTIAL RECITATIONS.

Collected by JAS. HENRY BROWNLEE. A timely book. Martial recitations, heroic, pathetic, humorous. The rarest gems of patriotic prose and poetry. Non-sectional, enthusing. 12mo; 232 pages; large, sharp type; excellent paper; silk cloth binding, gay and attractive. Price, **$1.00**; the same in handsome paper binding, 50 cents.

PRACTICAL LESSONS IN SCIENCE.

By Dr. J. T. SCOVELL, for ten years Professor of Natural Science in the Indiana State Normal School. Price, **$1.50**.

WOMAN, HER HOME, HEALTH AND BEAUTY.

A book that every lady should study and every household possess. An intensely interesting chapter on girlhood. Education of women. A very practical chapter on general hygiene, including hygiene of the skin and hygiene of the digestive organs. Sympathetic articles on motherhood and the hygiene of childhood. Also hygiene of the respiratory organs, hygiene of the eye, hygiene of the ear, hygiene of the generative organs. Cloth, **75 cents**; paper, **50 cents**.

For sale by all booksellers, or sent postpaid on receipt of advertised price.

THE WERNER COMPANY, Publishers,   -   Akron, O.

THE WERNER COMPANY'S PUBLICATIONS.

PRACTICAL LESSONS IN PSYCHOLOGY.
By WM. O. KROHN, Ph. D., Professor of Psychology and Pedagogy in the University of Illinois. Price $1.50.

KINGS OF THE PLATFORM AND PULPIT.
A hundred anecdotes of a hundred famous men,— our eminent orators, wits and sages. Who they are. How they have achieved fame. Their ups and downs in life,— Artemus Ward, Henry Ward Beecher, Josh Billings, John B. Gough, Petroleum V. Nasby, Robert J. Burdette, Dwight L. Moody, Robert G. Ingersoll, Bill Nye, Robert Collyer, Danbury News Man, T. DeWitt Talmage, Eli Perkins, Sam Jones, Geo. W. Peck, Wendell Phillips, Mrs. Partington, Prof. David Swing, Archdeacon Farrar, Bill Arp, etc. Large octavo volume, 7x10 inches; 600 pages; full of illustrations; fine paper; large, clear type; attractive binding. Cloth, plain edges. Price, $1.50.

LITTLE FOLKS' LIBRARY.
A set of six instructive and vastly entertaining midget volumes, written expressly for this library by carefully chosen authors. Illustrated by noted artists. Each book contains 128 pages, and from twenty to thirty-three full-page illustrations. The books are bound in Skytogan, are sewed, and have the appearance of "old folks "books in miniature.

RHYME UPON RHYME.
Edited by AMELIA HOFER, ex-president Kindergarten Department of National Educational Association. Illustrated by Harry O. Landers, of the Chicago *Times* staff.

LITTLE FARMERS.
By W. O. KROHN, Ph. D., Professor of Psychology, University of Illinois. Illustrated by Wm. Ottman.

CIRCUS DAY.
By GEORGE ADE, special writer for the Chicago *Record*. Illustrated by John T. McCutcheon.

FAIRY TALES.
From Shakespeare. By FAY ADAMS BRITTON, Shakespearian writer. Illustrated by Wm. Ottman. Vol. I. The Tempest; Vol. II. The Merchant of Venice. A Winter's Tale.

STORIES FROM HISTORY.
By JOHN HAZELDEN, historian. Illustrated by John T. McCutcheon, of the Chicago *Record* staff. Price, 50 cents per set.

BEAUTIFUL BRITAIN.
The scenery and splendors of the United Kingdom. Royal residences, palaces, castles, bowers, hunting lodges, river banks and islets, abbeys and halls, the homes of princes, views of noted places, historic landmarks and ancient ruins in the Lands of the Rose and Thistle. A magnificent collection of views, with elaborate descriptions and many interesting historical notes. Text set with emblematic borders, printed in a tint. A fine example of up-to-date printing. Large quarto volume, 11½x13½ inches, 385 pages, extra enameled paper. Extra English cloth, $4.50; half morocco, full gilt edges, $6.00; full morocco, full gilt edges, $7.50.

A VOYAGE IN THE YACHT SUNBEAM.
"Our home on the Ocean for Eleven Months." By LADY BRASSEY. The verdict of the public: "One of the most delightful and popular narratives of travel ever written. Both entertaining and instructive." For old and young alike. Size, 6x9 inches; 480 pages; many illustrations; extra quality paper. Cloth, gold stamped, $1.50; half morocco gold stamped, $2.00; full morocco, gold stamped, gilt edges, $2.50.

For sale by all booksellers, or sent postpaid on receipt of the advertised price.

THE WERNER COMPANY, Publishers, - Akron, O.

THE WERNER COMPANY'S PUBLICATIONS.

MAGNER'S STANDARD HORSE BOOK.

By D. MAGNER. The well-known authority on training, educating, taming and treating horses. The most complete work of the kind in existence; strongly endorsed by leading horse experts everywhere. Large quarto volume; 638 pages; over one thousand illustrations. Half Russia binding. Price, $2.50.

THE BIBLE FOR YOUNG PEOPLE.

In words of easy reading. The sweet stories of God's word. In the language of childhood. By the gifted author, JOSEPHINE POLLARD. Beautifully illustrated with nearly two hundred fifty striking original engravings and world-famous masterpieces of Sacred Art, and with magnificent colored plates. *The Bible For Young People* is complete in one sumptuous, massive, nearly square octavo volume, of over five hundred pages. Bound in extra cloth, ink and gold sides and back. $1.50.

GLIMPSES OF THE WORLD.

Hundreds of full-page views. Portraying scenes all over the world. The views composing this superb volume are reproduced by the perfected half-tone process from photographs collected by the celebrated traveler and lecturer, JOHN L. STODDARD, by whom the pictures are described in graphic language. In Glimpses of the World is presented a grand panorama of England, Scotland, and Ireland, France, Germany, Russia, Austria, Turkey, Italy, Spain, Asia, Africa, and North and South America. Unquestionably the finest work of the kind ever printed. Buckram. Price, $4.50.

THE WERNER POCKET ATLAS OF THE UNITED STATES.

A real pocket atlas 5x3½ inches, 96 pages, leatherette covers. Needed by every traveling man. Should be on every desk. Price, 10 cents.

THE CAPITOL COOK BOOK.

448 pages, 8½x6 inches; weight, 1½ pounds; over 1,400 tested recipes by HUGO ZIEMAN, ex-steward of the White House, and the well-known expert, Mrs. F. L. GILLETTE. Illustrated. Price, 50 cents.

THE WALDORF COOK BOOK.

By "OSCAR" of the Waldorf. The most thorough and complete treatise on Practical Cookery ever published. The author, OSCAR TSCHIRKY, Maitre d'Hotel, The Waldorf and Astoria, is acknowledged to be one of the foremost culinary authorities of the world. Elaborate directions are given for making ice creams, ices, pastries and tea and coffee. Selections may be made to gratify any taste. Original and varied recipes are given for making toothsome confections, preserves, jams, pickles and other condiments. Over 900 pages. Valuable information, indispensable to families, hotels, cafes and boarding houses. Wholesome, palatable, economic and systematic cooking. Everything used as food is fully considered. Nearly 4,000 recipes. The best and most comprehensive cook book compiled. Special features, such as suggestions with regard to the kitchen, menus, bills of fare, the seasons, market, etc., etc. Size, 8x10½ x 2¼ inches. Bound in one large octavo volume of over 900 pages in handsome oil cloth. Price, $2.50.

THE STORY OF AMERICAN HEROISM.

As told by the Medal Winners and Roll of Honor men. A remarkable collection of thrilling, historical incidents of personal adventures during and after the great Civil War. Narratives by such heroes as Gen. LEW WALLACE, Gen. O. O. HOWARD, Gen. ALEX. WEBB, Gen. FITZHUGH LEE, Gen. WADE HAMPTON. A war gallery of noted men and events. A massive volume of over 700 pages, printed on fine calendered paper. Illustrated with three hundred original drawings of personal exploits. English cloth, emblematic design in gold and colors, $2.50.

For sale by all booksellers, or sent postpaid on receipt of the advertised price.

THE WERNER COMPANY, Publishers, - Akron, O.

www.ingramcontent.com/pod-product-compliance
Lightning Source LLC
Chambersburg PA
CBHW020144170426
43199CB00010B/877